MY FIRST BOOK ABOUT...

LAS VEGAS!

Hello, little explorer!

Get ready to take a journey through the exciting history of Las Vegas. In this book, you'll discover how a quiet desert town became one of the most famous and fun places in the world.

Let's start our adventure and explore the wonders of Las Vegas!

A long time ago, Las Vegas was just a quiet desert.

Native people called the Paiutes lived here.

Las Vegas means 'the meadows' because there was water here.

Later, people came to live here and built a small town.

A big train track was built, and more people came.

Las Vegas became famous for its bright lights and big casinos.

The Las Vegas Strip is full of fun places to see!

Like Caesars Palace!

Paris Las Vegas!

And Circus Circus!

People love to watch shows and have fun in Las Vegas.

There are many fun things for families to do!

Las Vegas keeps growing and changing every day!

Las Vegas is a special place. Visit soon!

"Logan makes learning fun!"

www.LoganStover.com

Logan Stover is an Author, Historian, & Special Education Teacher from Southern California

Explore Logan's Other Books
Amazon - eBay - Etsy

Made in the USA
Monee, IL
26 October 2024

68700266R00021